CHAPTER 1

The United States – An Overview

The United States of America is the world's third largest country in terms of area (after Russia and Canada), and the world's most powerful country in terms of its economy and involvement in world affairs. The country was born in 1776, when American colonists declared themselves independent from Britain (see page 9). Since that time, the lure of a new life in the United States has attracted millions of immigrants from countries all over the world and today the United States has one of the most varied populations of any country. The United States' plentiful land, vast natural resources and the ideals and hard work of its citizens have helped to build the country that we know today – the world's only superpower.

The influence of the United States spreads far beyond its borders. It has used its military power to intervene in conflicts around the world, often defending or assisting communities in need. Its influence extends into the daily lives of billions of people who have benefited from the scientific advances and cultural richness of the United States. This includes developments in medicine and technology, but also in everyday products and services such as the global influence of Coca Cola or the worldwide popularity of American television programmes and Hollywood movies.

PHYSICAL EXTENT

The United States is a huge country – almost two-and-a-half times the area of the 27-member European Union, and 40 times the size of the United Kingdom (UK). It is made up of 50 states, two of which – the Hawaiian Islands in the South Pacific, and Alaska located to the northwest of Canada – are geographically separated from the other 48. Including Alaska, the United States has a northern border with

◀ Crowds on a pedestrian crossing in Manhattan, New York City. This snapshot of city life clearly displays the wide diversity of ethnic origin in the United States.

▲ School students say the Pledge of Allegiance to the US flag. The Pledge is as follows: 'I pledge allegiance to the Flag of the United States of America, and to the Republic for which it stands: one Nation under God, indivisible,with Liberty and Justice for all.'

Canada of 8,893 km (5,588 miles) while to its south it shares a border with Mexico of 3,141 km (1,952 miles). To the west of the United States is the Pacific Ocean and to the east lies the Atlantic Ocean, across which early settlers migrated from Europe. The Gulf of Mexico lies to the south of the United States along the Gulf States of Texas, Louisiana, Mississippi, Alabama and Florida.

RESOURCES

The United States straddles latitudes stretching from just above the Tropic of Cancer in the south to beyond the Arctic Circle in the north. This vast area encompasses a great diversity of landscapes and climates, and a variety of resources including timber, natural gas, uranium, copper and oil. The exploitation of these resources over the last four hundred years has allowed the United States to amass great wealth. However, in certain areas of the United States, the use of resources has led to considerable damage to natural environments.

As well as exploiting its own resources the United States also imports resources from abroad, especially where its own supplies are exhausted or depleted. It is particularly dependent on oil imports. In 2007 the United States consumed 20.68 million barrels of oil per day, 59 per cent of which were imported. This trade in resources is just one element of the diverse and complex trading relationships that the United States has with countries around the world.

MILITARY POWER

The immense wealth of the United States has given it great military power, and it has been involved in most of the major world conflicts over the last 90 years. However, its role on the world stage has aroused deep antagonism amongst some groups of people, making the country a target for extremist action. On 11 September 2001, terrorist attacks on the World Trade Center, New York and the Pentagon in Washington D.C. left more than 3,000 people dead. At present, the United States is involved in trying to bring democratic government to Iraq, and also in negotiating a peaceful solution between Israel and the Palestinians in the Middle East. The Middle East region contains 62 per cent of the Earth's proven oil reserves and is an important supplier to many countries including the United States. The United States' role in the Middle East helps to ensure the regular flow of oil on to the world markets, a flow that could be halted by political instability or conflict in the region.

The United States continues to draw large numbers of migrants to its shores, attracted by the religious and political freedoms the country offers them, and by the economic opportunities of employment or of starting their own businesses. This influx of people continually adds to the multicultural population of the United States and helps to give the country a powerful and exciting energy.

Did you know?

One of the most powerful symbols of the United States, the Statue of Liberty which stands in New York Harbor, was a gift from the people of France in 1886. It represents political and individual freedoms.

Physical geography

- Land area: 9,158,960 sq km/ 3,536,274 sq miles
- Water area: 470,131 sq km/ 181,518 sq miles
- Total area: 9,629,091 sq km/ 3,717,792 sq miles
- World rank (by area): 3
- Land boundaries: 12,034 km/ 7,473 miles
- Border countries: Canada, Mexico
- Coastline: 19,924 km/ 12,373 miles
- Highest point: Mount McKinley (6,194 m/ 20,322 ft)

Lowest point: Death Valley (-86 m/ -282 ft)

Source: CIA World Factbook

◀ New York City firefighters raise the American flag at the site of the World Trade Center on 11 September 2001.

CANADA
UNITED STATES OF AMERICA
MEXICO
PACIFIC OCEAN
ATLANTIC OCEAN
Gulf of Mexico
ROCKY MOUNTAINS
GREAT PLAINS
Washington, D.C.
New York City
Philadelphia
Chicago
Los Angeles
Houston
San Diego
Phoenix
Dallas
San Antonio
Detroit
WASHINGTON
OREGON
CALIFORNIA
NEVADA
IDAHO
MONTANA
WYOMING
UTAH
ARIZONA
COLORADO
NEW MEXICO
NORTH DAKOTA
SOUTH DAKOTA
NEBRASKA
KANSAS
OKLAHOMA
TEXAS
MINNESOTA
IOWA
MISSOURI
ARKANSAS
LOUISIANA
WISCONSIN
ILLINOIS
MICHIGAN
INDIANA
OHIO
KENTUCKY
TENNESSEE
MISSISSIPPI
ALABAMA
GEORGIA
FLORIDA
SOUTH CAROLINA
NORTH CAROLINA
VIRGINIA
WEST VIRGINIA
PENNSYLVANIA
NEW YORK
MAINE
VERMONT
NEW HAMPSHIRE
MASSACHUSETTS
RHODE ISLAND
CONNECTICUT
NEW JERSEY
DELAWARE
MARYLAND
Lake Superior
Lake Michigan
Lake Huron
Lake Erie
Lake Ontario
Mississippi
Missouri
Rio Grande
Colorado
Mississippi Delta
Florida Keys
BAHAMAS
ALASKA
BROOKS RANGE
Mount McKinley 6,194m
Anchorage
RUSS. FED.
Gulf of Alaska
400 km
400 miles
HAWAII
Kauai
Oahu
Molokai
Maui
Lanai
Hawaii
Honolulu
100 km
100 miles
500 kilometres
500 miles
Legend
Capital
Cities > 2,000,000
Cities > 1,000,000
Cities > 500,000
Other cities
Mountain

CHAPTER 2

History

EARLY BEGINNINGS

The first humans to inhabit the land that was to become the United States were the ancestors of today's Native Americans. Most theories suggest that they migrated across a landbridge between Asia and America more than 10,000 years ago, when sea levels were much lower. Once in the Americas, they gradually spread south, forming many different tribes. European colonization of this land began with the voyage of the Italian-born, Spanish navigator, Christopher Columbus, who landed in the Caribbean in 1492. By the 17th century, people from Spain, France, England and the Netherlands had colonized large areas of this 'New World'.

THE WAR OF INDEPENDENCE

By 1763, Britain controlled Canada and all of North America east of the Mississippi River. However, many of the people living in Britain's American colonies had begun to question their treatment by the British government. The colonists were expected to feed and house British troops in the colonies, which was a heavy drain on their incomes. Britain levied heavy taxes on the colonists, including taxes on many goods that needed to be imported such as sugar, coffee, tea and wine. Many colonists resented paying these taxes, particularly as they had no representation in the British Parliament in return. The War of Independence began in 1775 when many

Did you know?

Thanksgiving, held every year in the United States on the fourth Thursday in November, has its origins in the festival to give thanks for the safe gathering of the harvest by early English settlers in North America.

► Modern-day Americans take part in a re-enactment of the first Thanksgiving in Plymouth, Massachusetts, when Native Americans and settlers joined together to give thanks for a successful harvest.

▶ In this detail of a painting by John Trumbull (1756-1843), representatives of the 13 colonies sign the Declaration of Independence on 4 July 1776.

colonists decided to break free from British rule. During this war, the Declaration of Independence was drawn up and signed by representatives of the 13 British colonies on 4 July 1776, now regarded as the founding date of the United States of America. The British sent troops to prevent the colonies enacting this declaration, but the British eventually lost the war, surrendering in Yorktown, Virginia, in 1781.

THE NEW NATION

The Articles of Confederation, drawn up in 1781, saw the colonies attempt to work together as the United States of America, but these Articles failed to establish an effective federal government. In 1787, the Articles were abandoned and a new Constitution was written. The aim of this Constitution, and the Bill of Rights that followed in 1791 (see page 22), was to safeguard individual freedoms and to organize the country without giving too much power to a centralized government. The first president to head the government was George Washington, who, in 1789, was unanimously elected by representatives from all the states.

EXPANDING WESTWARDS

During the first half of the 19th century, the United States expanded steadily westwards across the North American continent. In 1803, the US government bought Louisiana from the French, extending its territories as far west as the Rocky Mountains. But as American settlers moved west they came into conflict with the Native Americans who had lived on these lands for thousands of years. The US government sent troops to deal with the Native Americans, and many had their lands taken away by force. In 1838, the 15,000 members of the Cherokee tribe were ordered to leave their lands in Georgia and make the 1,600-km (1,000-mile) journey to Oklahoma. About 4,000 Cherokee died on this terrible march, which came to be known as the 'Trail of Tears'.

FREE AND SLAVE STATES

Black slaves imported from Africa had been put to work in America since the middle of the 17th century. However, slavery was at odds with the statement in the Declaration of Independence that 'all men are created equal', and many Americans, known as abolitionists, called for the end of slavery. By the early 19th century, all northern states ('free' states) had outlawed slavery, but in the southern states ('slave' states), which relied on slave labour for work on the plantations, the right to keep slaves was fiercely protected. In government, a balance between free states and slave states was struck, but in 1820 a new state called Missouri applied to be admitted to the United States as a slave-owning state. In order to avoid increasing the representation of the slave states in government, the Missouri Compromise was created to allow for the admission of both Missouri as a slave state and the newly created state of Maine in the north as a free state. For a short time, this arrangement gave a balance of power between the two factions.

THE CIVIL WAR

The compromise between free and slave states came under pressure after the end of the Mexican-American War of 1848. Under the treaty that ended the war, the United States gained large areas of territory in the southwest, but the question arose about whether the new states created out of this territory should be free or slave states. After years of attempted compromise and disagreements, matters came to a head in 1861 when 11 southern states left the Union (the United States) to form the Confederacy after the election of President Abraham Lincoln (1809-65), who was an opponent of slavery. Despite Lincoln's attempts to keep the states together, this split was the beginning of a bloody Civil War between the northern (Union) and southern (Confederate) states. The Union emerged victorious in 1865, and, with the addition of the 13th Amendment to the Constitution, slavery was outlawed throughout the United States. It was to be many more years, however, before descendants of the freed slaves were given full civil rights.

▶ This photograph, taken in June 1862, shows four Union soldiers grouped around their cannon near Fair Oaks, Virginia. The Union Army fought for the northern states in the American Civil War.

BEGINNING OF THE MODERN NATION

After the end of Civil War, the Industrial Revolution in the United States resulted in the country's rapid development into an important industrial power with major oil, textile, steel and mining industries. America's world influence through manufactured goods had begun. Its role as a major world power also grew with its support of the Allies (Britain, France, Russia and Italy) in World War I.

After the war, America's economy suffered a major setback in 1929 with the financial collapse of the New York Stock Market on Wall Street. The value of the dollar fell and overnight people's savings became worthless. High unemployment and rapidly rising prices led to a period in the 1930s known as the Great Depression which ended only when the United States entered World War II in support of the European Allies (Britain and the Commonwealth, France and Russia) after the bombing by Japan of Pearl Harbor in 1941. To supply the war effort, factories were put into full production to supply arms, vehicles and food, resulting in a doubling of manufacturing output and a rapid reduction in unemployment. The United States fought with the Allies in Europe against Hitler and his armies and also in the Pacific against Japan. Nearly 300,000 US soldiers lost their lives during these conflicts. In 1945, the United States dropped atomic bombs on the Japanese cities of Hiroshima and Nagasaki, which ended the war in the Pacific, but had devastating and long-lasting effects on the Japanese.

▼ Hunger marchers in front of the Capitol building, Washington D.C. in 1932, during the Great Depression. Over 12,000 people made the long journey from Pittsburgh, Pennsylvania.

THE COLD WAR

After World War II, the United States became a founding member of the United Nations (UN) and took a lead role in world politics. America felt that communism, especially as practised by the former Soviet Union, was a serious threat to world peace. There was great political hostility between the two countries but as there was no direct military conflict this period became known as the 'Cold War'. However, the United States was involved in two wars intended to prevent the spread of communism. The first was the Korean War (1950-3) the result of which was the division of the country, which remains today, into communist North Korea and democratic South Korea. From the early 1960s, there was the much longer involvement in the war in Vietnam. America gave support, including troops, to South Vietnam in its fight against pro-communist forces from North Vietnam. Increasing costs in terms of money and lives, and the fact that this was the first time that television cameras had brought the reality of war into people's homes, led to many Americans protesting against the war. The Vietnam war ended in 1973 after a settlement and the withdrawal of US troops.

THE IMPORTANCE OF OIL

After World War II the United States became increasingly dependent on oil to fuel its industries, transport and homes. In 1973, in

Focus on: The civil rights movement

The movement to bring full civil rights and equality to African-Americans started in the 19th century, but even after World War II education and public transport in some southern states remained segregated by race. A campaign of protests and boycotts throughout the 1950s and '60s resulted in desegregation and important legislation to end racial discrimination. In the 1960s, the famous civil rights campaigner Martin Luther King spoke of his dream of a country where all would live together in peace. He was assassinated in 1968. Today, the civil rights movement continues to work to end racial discrimination at all levels of US society.

▲ Martin Luther King waves from the Lincoln Memorial, Washington D.C., to people taking part in a civil rights march held on 28 August 1963.

▲ A US soldier stands on a destroyed Iraqi tank in 1991, during the Gulf War. In the background can be seen the fires from the Kuwaiti oil wells that were set alight by Saddam Hussein's retreating Iraqi army.

retaliation against the West's support of the state of Israel, the Arab states cut off oil supplies to the USA, Japan and Western Europe. This crisis highlighted the importance to the United States of the oil supply from the countries of the Middle East. When Iraq invaded Kuwait in 1990, the United States, along with other countries, fought to liberate the country and keep Kuwait's considerable oil reserves accessible.

THE 'WAR ON TERROR'

With the break-up of the Soviet Union in 1991, the United States became the world's only superpower. This position of global dominance has created some powerful enemies, particularly in the Arab world where groups such as Al-Qaeda have become increasingly militant in resisting America's influence. The terrorist attacks in 2001 (see page 6) prompted the president of the United States, George W. Bush, to declare a 'war on terror' and, late in the same year, the United States with the help of several other countries took action against terrorist forces in Afghanistan. However, several countries expressed strong disapproval of the US-led invasion of Iraq that took place in 2003 and toppled the regime of Saddam Hussein. Today, the United States is still involved, with the UK and other countries, in trying to establish democratic government in Iraq, but its actions have been questioned by many people around the world, including many Americans who resent the loss of young American lives during the conflict and believe the government's case for going to war was weak.

CHAPTER 3

Landscape and Climate

The United States covers 9,158,960 sq km (3,536,274 sq miles) and incorporates many different landscapes. The country has two main mountain ranges. The Appalachians are located in the east of the country and include the Blue Ridge Mountains. In the west are the great mountains of the Rockies that include several peaks over 4,000 m (13,120 feet). Between these two mountain ranges lie the Great Plains, where altitude rarely reaches 400 m (1,312 ft). Many rivers drain this area including the Mississippi and its tributaries. Alaska, lying to the northwest of Canada, contains the tallest peak in the United States, Mount McKinley at 6,194 m (20,322 feet). Hawaii, separated from the mainland of the United States by 3,840 km (2,385 miles) of ocean, consists of 132 volcanic islands, seven of which are inhabited. It still has active volcanoes, including Mauna Loa which is 9,170 m (30,080 feet) high from the seabed, making it the highest mountain in the world when measured in this way.

NATURAL HAZARDS

The United States experiences a wide range of natural hazards including tornadoes, wildfires, hurricanes, avalanches, flooding, earthquakes and volcanic eruptions. Most of the large tornadoes occur in Texas, Oklahoma, Kansas

▼ Fresh snowfall on Mount McKinley, the highest mountain in the United States, located in Denali National Park in Alaska.

and Nebraska along an area called 'Tornado Alley'. They are very destructive and each year cause about 60 deaths. Tropical cyclones, known as hurricanes, make landfall in Florida and other southern and southeastern states. The Atlantic hurricane season runs from June to November, while the hurricane season for the eastern Pacific is May to November. The National Weather Service issues regular reports and warnings about hurricanes.

Most earthquakes and volcanoes occur near the margins of the tectonic plates that form the earth's surface. Earthquakes are common in California because of the San Andreas fault which marks the boundary between two of these plates, and which runs through the state. In 1994, a huge earthquake struck Los Angeles in southern California, killing 60 people and injuring more than 7,000. The earthquake measured 6.6 on the Richter scale. The most spectacular recent volcanic eruption in the United States took place in the Cascade Mountains in the northwest of the country, in 1980. The perfect cone-shape of Mount St. Helens was blown to pieces when the volcano erupted on 18 May, removing 2.7 cubic km (0.65 cubic miles) of its top to leave a vast crater. Forests were flattened by the blast for 600 sq km (230 square miles) and the ash cloud from the blast closed Seattle airport and cut out sunlight over the city of Seattle for several days. Fifty-seven people died as a result of the eruption.

Did you know?

The Great Lakes in the north of the United States contain one-fifth of the world's fresh water.

Focus on: Hurricane Katrina

Hurricane Katrina made landfall in Louisiana on 29 August 2005 with windspeeds of up to 320 km per hour (200 mph). It devastated an area of the southern United States the size of Great Britain. Much of the city of New Orleans is below sea level and when the levees (dykes) that surround the city broke, two-thirds of the city was flooded. Many people evacuated the city, but those who were unable to leave were stranded for several days without food or clean water. It is estimated that 1,698 deaths were caused by Hurricane Katrina, and US$200 billion dollars, worth of damage to property and businesses.

▲ Following Hurricane Katrina in September 2005, a volunteer rescues residents from a local school in Baton Rouge, Louisiana, where they had gone to escape their flooded homes.

▲ Badwater, the lowest point in America, is part of Death Valley National Park and attracts thousands of tourists every year to view its stark landscapes.

CONTRASTING CLIMATES

Climates in the United States range from the tropical to the arctic. Hawaii, in the South Pacific, has a tropical climate that is hot all year round with the average temperature never falling below 23°C (73°F) and a wet season from October to March. This contrasts with Alaska where almost a third of the state is inside the Arctic Circle. During December, Alaska has only one hour of daylight and temperatures average -23°C (-9°F). In fact, the average temperature only rises above freezing point for seven months of the year, too cold in most parts for trees to grow.

Did you know?

The highest temperature ever recorded in the United States was 57°C (134°F), in Death Valley, California, in 1913. The lowest temperature ever recorded was -62°C (-80°F) at Prospect Creek in Alaska, in 1971.

Within the 48 states of the continental United States, climates range from hot desert, through arid grasslands to moist coastal and forest areas. Climates along the coasts are milder than inland because the sea moderates temperatures, preventing them from becoming either very hot or very cold. Florida has a warm, subtropical climate that allows the cultivation of oranges, lemons and other fruits. California, in the west, has a Mediterranean-type climate with hot, dry summers and mild, damp winters. This climate is ideal for growing grapes and supports an important Californian wine industry. Inland and away from the influence of the sea, states such as Nebraska and Kansas experience very cold winters and very hot summers. This is the prairie region, one of the world's most important wheat-growing areas.

The Rocky Mountains in the west block the path of rain-bearing westerly winds, forcing them to rise and drop their rain. In Oregon and Washington, the heavy rainfall helps large forests to grow. The eastern side of the Rockies is much drier. The Mojave and Sonoran deserts lie in the southwest, where temperatures are higher. Here vegetation includes cacti and other plant species such as blackbrush that have adapted to the hot, arid conditions.

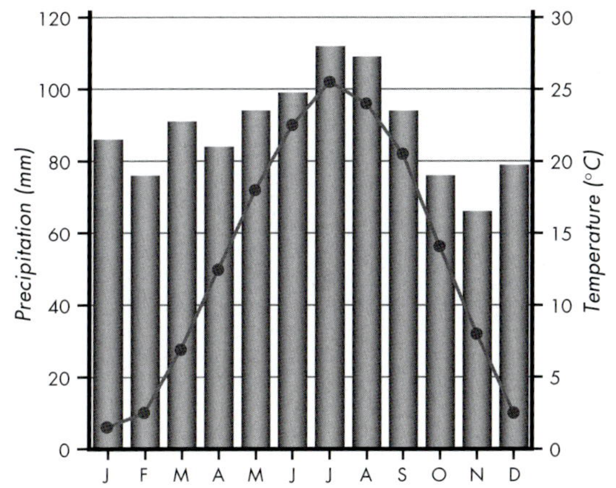

▲ Average monthly climate conditions in Washington D.C.

▼ Tourists look out from the South Rim across the Grand Canyon in Arizona, one of the natural wonders of the world.

Focus on: The Grand Canyon

In the Grand Canyon, the Colorado River has cut a gorge 1.5 km (1 mile) deep through many different layers of rock. Travelling down from the top of the canyon to the river you pass through four different vegetation and climate zones, from forests of Douglas Fir down to desert at the bottom. It can be snowing at the rim and hot enough for T-shirts at the bottom, with a difference of 15°C (30°F)! In fact, the range of environments in the Grand Canyon is similar to those you would encounter driving 2,000 km (1,243 miles) from Canada to New Mexico!

CHAPTER 4

Population and Settlements

The United States is the world's third most populous nation, with 304 millon people. However, its population is unevenly distributed. The most densely populated region is the northeast, with an average of 438 people per sq km (1,134 people per sq mile) in the state of New Jersey, compared to an average of just over 2 people per sq km (6 people per square mile) in Montana. The states of California, in the west, and Florida, in the southeast, have also attracted large concentrations of people, partly because of their pleasant climates and coastal positions. Only 20 per cent of the US population lives in rural areas, and only 10 per cent of this rural population lives on a farm, with the rest in small settlements.

AN AGEING POPULATION

The population of the United States is ageing – in 2008, 13 per cent of Americans were over 65 years of age, and by 2030 this figure is expected to rise to 20 per cent. Life expectancy has increased from 66 in 1960 to 75 in 2008 for men, and from 73 to 81 in the same period for women. Although the birth rate is high for a developed country, especially in young immigrant families, the government has estimated that without further immigration there will be a shortage of workers by 2026, due to a high proportion of the present working population reaching retirement age.

Population data

- Population: 304 million
- Population 0-14 yrs: 20%
- Population 15-64 yrs: 67%
- Population 65+ yrs: 13%
- Population growth rate: 0.9%
- Population density: 30.9 per sq km/ 80.1 per sq mile
- Urban population: 80%
- Major cities: New York 19,040,000
  Los Angeles 12,500,000
  Chicago 8,990,000

Source: United Nations and World Bank

◀ Increasing life expectancy in the United States means more active years in retirement, and an ageing population.

MIGRATION

Many of the African-Americans who today make up 12.7 per cent of the US population are descendants of slaves taken from their homelands in the 17th and 18th centuries. However, until the early years of the 20th century, most migrants came to the United States from Europe, initially from countries in northern Europe such as Britain, Ireland, Germany and Sweden, later from countries in southern and eastern Europe, particularly Italy. Two million Jews migrated to the United States between 1880 and 1920 as they fled persecution in Russia and Germany. During the 20th century, increasing numbers of migrants arrived from Asia and South America. Americans who originated from Spanish-speaking countries of South America and the Caribbean are known as Hispanics. Today, the Hispanic community is the fastest-growing minority in the United States. The US Census Bureau estimates that the high birth rate in the Hispanic community, as well as continued immigration, will see the Hispanic share of the US population almost double by 2050, from 12.6 per cent to 24.4 per cent.

Between 1970 and 2006 the number of well-educated Indians who had migrated to the United States increased over 30 times to 1.5 million. Many were attracted by job opportunities in high-tech industries where American companies are having problems in recruiting workers. These new migrants have brought fresh ideas and enthusiasm, and are an important resource for the country. However, the Asian population of the United States includes people originating not only from India but also from Pakistan, the countries of southeast Asia, Korea, China and Japan. They make up the second fastest-growing sector of the US population and are overwhelmingly concentrated in just three states: New York, California and Hawaii.

Focus on: Illegal immigration

The United States' border with Mexico is often referred to as 'leaky', as it is impossible to police all 3,141 km (1,952 miles). Illegal Mexican migrants take great risks by trying to cross the desert landscape to enter the United States. But Mexico is a less developed and poorer country than the United States, so many Mexicans are prepared to take the gamble of crossing the border in search of job opportunities and better pay.

▲ An English class for immigrants in Arlington, Virginia. Learning English is seen as vitally important by most immigrants to the United States – and by the US government which helps to fund many courses.

? *Did you know?*

Los Angeles is home to 20 per cent of the Hispanic population of the United States.

URBAN AMERICA

The United States' population is largely urban, with 80 per cent of people living in towns and cities. In 2007, the United States had 40 cities with populations of over one million. The fastest growing cities are in the southwest and include Phoenix (Arizona), Los Angeles (California) and San Antonio (Texas).

City centres often have high levels of air and noise pollution, traffic congestion and crime. Widespread car ownership means that large numbers of people choose to live outside the city centres and commute long distances to work, resulting in urban sprawl as low-density suburbs are built on the edges of cities. The suburbs are particularly popular with middle-class Americans seeking a better quality of life. Land is cheaper away from city centres, so many people can afford individual houses with backyards (gardens), rather than small city flats. Many jobs and retail outlets have also moved out to the city edges, causing further decentralization.

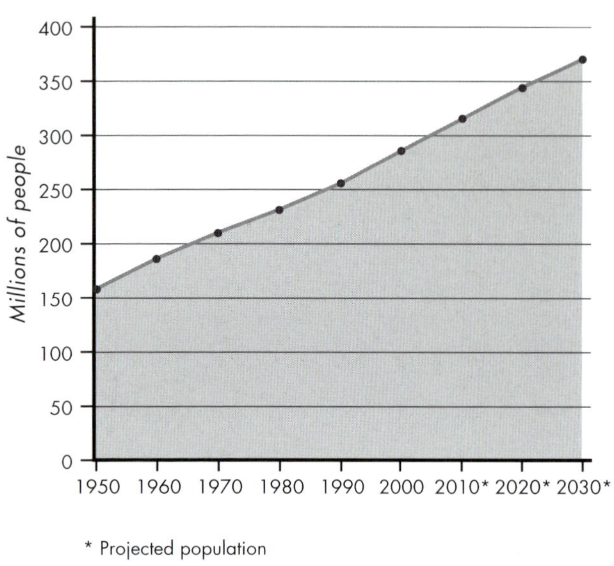

▲ Population growth 1950-2030

POVERTY AND SETTLEMENT

Although it is the world's wealthiest country, poverty can be found across most parts of the the United States with some of the poorest communities being in largely rural states such as West Virginia and Mississippi. However, the greatest concentration of poverty is found in US cities, for example in Chicago, Detroit, Los Angeles and New York. In the deprived areas of these cities, it is common for residents (many of them recent immigrants to the United States) to have difficulties in getting jobs and a good education, leaving them feeling alienated from the rest of society.

Occasionally tensions build up in city areas between different communities, or between residents and police. For example, in 1992, there were riots in Los Angeles after a mostly white jury acquitted four policeman of beating

▼ A massive surburban development stretches into the desert on the edge of Las Vegas, Nevada.

a black motorist, Rodney King. Although the trial verdict was the spark that set off the riots, tensions had long been building between the African-American, Hispanic and Korean communities in the southern districts of Los Angeles. Providing equal opportunities for all people, regardless of race or ethnicity, is vitally important to help relieve such tensions and to promote the integration of communities in America's cities.

Did you know?

The most populous state in the United States is California. With 36 million people it has 12 per cent of the population living in 4 per cent of the total land area. The most populous city is New York City, with just over 19 million people.

▼ African-Americans in Harlem, New York City, America's most famous black community.

Focus on: Harlem

Harlem, in New York City, is a largely deprived area where most residents are of African-American descent. In the past it has been known for its high crime levels and poorly maintained housing, but today there are many projects that aim to improve the area and offer new opportunities to its residents. One example is the redevelopment of a run-down manufacturing area in West Harlem by Columbia University, which will offer a range of jobs both during and after construction. Another is the Carmel Hill Project which is renovating decayed buildings, setting up tenants' groups and providing improved access to services such as health care and education.

CHAPTER 5

Government and Politics

The United States is a federal republic with a long history of democracy. The people of the United States vote for the leaders who they think will best represent them in the government. The basis of government in the United States is the Constitution, drawn up in 1787. The writers of the Constitution created three branches of government that would balance and check each other; the executive, the judicial and the legislative. Just four years later, in 1791, ten amendments were added to the Constitution which are known as the Bill of Rights. The aim of these amendments was to set out more clearly the rights of the individual citizen, including the three important rights of freedom of speech, freedom of the press, and freedom to follow any chosen religion. The Bill also laid down the right for every citizen to bear arms and to have a trial by jury if accused of a crime.

GOVERNMENT OF THE UNITED STATES

The executive branch of government is headed by the president of the United States and is in charge of enforcing the laws passed by the legislative branch. It includes many departments, such as education and agriculture.

▼ Capitol Hill, Washington D.C. is the home of the US government. The Capitol building was begun in 1793 and was designed to house the Congress of the United States (see page 23).

▲ President George W. Bush stands in the famous Oval Office at the White House, in Washington D.C., just after his election victory in 2004.

The judicial branch of the government acts as a check on the executive and legislative arms in order to ensure they do not violate the Constitution. The judicial branch also includes the highest court in the land, the Supreme Court, which has the power to question whether a law or an action by the government goes against the Constitution. It also has power over the other federal courts.

The legislative branch makes the laws that run the country. This is done in Congress which is made up of two houses, the House of Representatives and the Senate. The House of Representatives has 435 members. The number is based on the size of the population of a state, so, for example, New Hampshire (with a low population) has two representatives while Louisiana (with a high population) has seven. The Senate has 100 members with two senators from every state. The main aim of Congress is to draw up, debate and pass bills that will eventually become law. However, if the president does not agree with a particular bill it is returned to Congress for further discussion.

POLITICAL PARTIES

There are two main parties in the United States: the Republicans and the Democrats. The Republicans are viewed as conservative and traditional while the Democrats are thought of as more liberal and progressive. Inside each party, there is a wide range of views. Representatives do not always follow the party line and may vote with the opposition. It is possible to have a president from one party and a majority in Congress from another. This can make passing new laws very difficult.

Did you know?

The symbol of the Republican Party is an elephant and that of the Democratic Party is a donkey.

FEDERAL AND STATE GOVERNMENT

The national, overall government of the United States is known as the federal government. Individual states also have authority to set their own laws and constitutions to take account of local conditions as long as they don't conflict with federal law. States can make their own laws in areas such as education, criminal justice and hospital organization. Differences between the laws of various states can cause confusion. For example, in Montana, a fifteen-year-old can have a full driver's licence, but in some states a driver cannot be fully licensed until 18.

ELECTIONS AND THE CITIZEN

Presidential elections take place every four years, and a president can stay in office for a maximum of two terms, or eight years. A presidential campaign normally begins at least a year ahead of the election, and money has to be raised in order to finance it. The presidential candidate will work hard to create a positive

▼ Voters at a polling station in Burbank, California, mark their ballot papers in a state election in November 2005.

impression on the electorate by making good use of the media, including radio, magazines, newspapers but above all, television. Senators are elected every six years and representatives every two years. Every citizen over the age of 18 is entitled to vote (with a few exceptions such as convicted criminals and those who are judged to be mentally incompetent), and in the United States voting is viewed as a civic duty.

People from foreign countries who are living in the United States can apply to become US citizens via a process called naturalization. The requirements for naturalization include being of good character, loyal to the United States and willing to take the Oath of Allegiance. The person applying for naturalization must also be able to read, write and understand basic English. Being a US citizen involves responsibilities as well as rights. Citizens are expected to pay their taxes. Young men are also required to register to be called up for military service if necessary, although the government has not used this power since the early 1970s.

Focus on: Capital punishment

There are 38 US states where a criminal can receive the death penalty and 12 where they cannot. Between 1976 and August 2008, 1099 people have been executed in the United States. However, over the last 35 years, 125 people have been found innocent (or freed from blame) whilst waiting on death row. In 2005, California had over 600 criminals waiting on death row to be executed – more than any other state. Since 1982 13 people in California have been executed, compared to over 350 in Texas, three times more than in any other state.

◀ A woman takes the Oath of Allegiance, the last stage in becoming a naturalized citizen of the United States, at a ceremony in Broward County Convention Center, Florida, September 2000.

CHAPTER 6

Energy and Resources

The United States has a wealth of natural resources that includes minerals, forests, fish, land and water. It also benefits from some of the world's largest reserves of oil, coal and gas for energy. Despite this, the United States has insufficient energy resources to meet the demands of its population without imports.

ENERGY RESOURCES

The American lifestyle is energy-hungry. Many homes are centrally heated in winter, air-conditioned in summer and have numerous labour-saving machines and gadgets, all of which depend on energy. In addition many people in the United States are dependent on their cars for transport, while others use their cars as a matter of choice.

Did you know?

There were 50 per cent more cars on the road in the United States in 2005 than in the 1970s, but today's cars are more fuel-efficient.

In 2006, the economy of the United States consumed over 20 million barrels of oil a day but produced only eight million barrels. The shortfall in supply is made up by oil imports from Canada, the Middle East, West Africa and Central and South America. The Middle East supplies around 20 per cent of the oil used in the United States.

The majority (a third) of coal mined in the United States comes from the central state of Wyoming. The United States is self-sufficient in coal, and coal is the main fuel for electricity production, providing 51 per cent of national output. The United States produces natural gas as a fuel, but it has to import gas from Canada in order to keep up with consumption. There are 489,600 km (304,200 miles) of gas pipeline across the country, distributing the fuel. Nuclear power produces 20 per cent of the United States' electricity from 104 reactors. Although there are concerns about the disposal of nuclear wastes, nuclear power neither produces greenhouse gases nor contributes to global climate change.

◀ Oil is pumped from oil-bearing rocks beneath a golf course in Houston, Texas.

Other alternatives to fossil fuels include hydroelectric (HEP), solar, tidal, wind and geothermal power. In southern states such as California and Florida, where there are long hours of sunshine, banks of photovoltaic panels harness the sunlight and are used to generate electricity. Wind generation still accounts for only two per cent of electricity produced by renewable means, but it is the fastest growing sector. The wind farm at the San Gorgonio Mountain Pass, California, has over 4,000 turbines and generates enough electricity for the town of Palm Springs and its surrounding area. The newest turbines are 93 metres (305 feet) tall – almost the height of the Statue of Liberty – and can each provide electricity for 500 homes.

▲ The vast wind farm at San Gorgonio, California, provides a clean, non-polluting energy source as it harnesses moving air in the mountain pass.

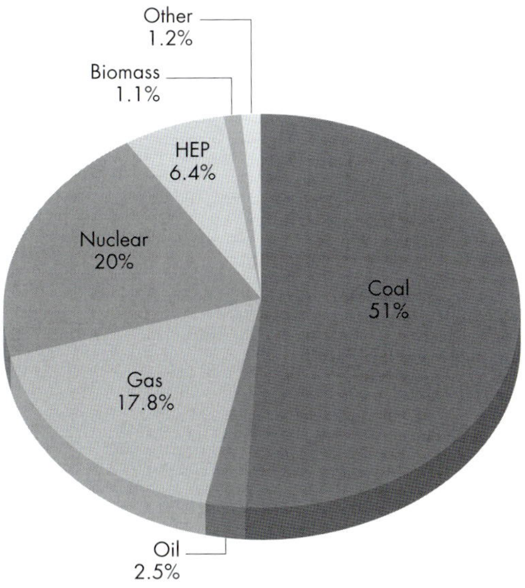

▲ Electricity production by type

Focus on: Hydrogen-fuelled cars

Every year, the United States produces nine million tons of hydrogen which is used in industry, and as a rocket fuel by NASA (the National Aeronautics and Space Administration). However, in the future it could be used to fuel cars, and hydrogen fuel cells are being developed in US universities in partnership with car companies. The great advantage is that these cars will have almost zero emissions, but one problem is the huge expense of converting petrol stations to providing hydrogen.

Did you know?

A little over two-thirds of the oil (67 per cent) consumed in the United States is used by the transport sector.

METALS AND MINERALS

The United States mines large amounts of a variety of metals and minerals and is the second biggest producer of copper ore, after Chile. Nearly all (99 per cent) copper production is in the three states of Arizona, Utah and New Mexico in the southwest. The United States produces large amounts of aluminium, a third of which comes from recycled aluminium metal. The same is true of lead, where 75 per cent of lead production is from recycled car batteries and only 25 per cent is newly mined. The United States produces a fifth of the world's sulphur, which is mined mainly along the coasts of Texas and Louisiana, and is used in the manufacture of chemicals.

FORESTS AND FISHING

About 33 per cent of the United States is covered with forest, with large areas of forest on the western side of the nation. Most of the western forest is federally owned and nearly a quarter of it is protected. In contrast, 83 per cent of the forests of the eastern side are privately owned, and this is where most of the timber harvesting occurs.

▼ At Port Sulphur, on the Louisiana coast, sulphur is pumped from underground mines using high-pressure hot water and is then left to cool and solidify.

During 2006 over 4 million tonnes (4.19 tons) of fish were landed in the United States. The most productive area is Alaska where 58 per cent of the catch is landed, followed by Louisiana, where the catch is 10 per cent of the total.

WATER RESOURCES

The United States has several large rivers including the Mississippi, which is the country's longest river at 6,019 km (3,740 miles) and drains a total of 4,160 square km (1,606 square miles). The southwest of the country is arid, yet it has cities with large populations such as Las Vegas, Phoenix and Los Angeles which require vast amounts of water. Los Angeles takes up 6 per cent of the land area of California, and is home to 45 per cent of the state's population, yet it has only 0.6 per cent of the state's river flow and is dependent on piping in water from distant locations, thereby altering river ecosystems and reducing water resources for other settlements.

Energy data

- Energy consumption as % of world total: 23.4%
- Energy consumption by sector (% of total):

Industry:	24.3%
Transportation:	40.8%
Agriculture:	0.9%
Services:	12.4%
Residential:	17.2%
Other:	4.4%

- CO_2 emissions as % of world total: 20.6%
- CO_2 emissions per capita in tonnes p.a.:7.6

Source: World Resources Institute

Focus on: The Colorado

The Colorado River (its name means 'red river') rises in the Rockies and passes through much of the arid southwest. It is an important resource for the communities along its route as a drinking water supply, irrigation source and a producer of HEP. In fact, nearly all of its water is used up in the United States before it reaches the Gulf of California in Mexico. This has led to tensions between Mexico and the United States, as the Mexicans feel they should be able to use some of the river's water as a resource.

▶ Fish being weighed at the old Fulton Street Fish Market in New York City.

CHAPTER 7

Economy and Income

The United States is an advanced industrialized nation with an enormous service sector (accounting for around 76 per cent of employment) and a highly productive manufacturing sector. As manufacturing has become more automated it has required fewer workers and the number now working in manufacturing has fallen to just 22 per cent of the workforce. Agriculture in the United States accounts for only 2 per cent of employment and is a highly mechanized and efficient industry. All of this activity makes the United States the wealthiest nation in the world – yet more than 12 per cent of the population lives in poverty, and the divide between the wealthy and the poor is growing.

THE MARKET ECONOMY

The economy of the United States is based on free enterprise and the market economy. This means that the majority of business decisions are made by private companies and individuals rather than by the government. The lack of government regulations on businesses gives them greater flexibility than in many other countries and encourages the growth of both businesses and the wider economy. However, the market economy does not cover all aspects of life, and most people are happy for the government to oversee areas such as education and national defence. The government also acts as a regulator in, for example, checking food standards in shops and restaurants.

Did you know?

The biggest and most powerful companies in the United States have revenues many times larger than the poorest countries of the world. For example Wal-Mart Stores had revenues of US$351 billion and General Motors US$207 billion in 2007, compared to the GNI of a country such as Ethiopia (US$17.6 billion) or Nepal (US$9.7 billion).

▶ The home of a former cotton picker in Tehula, Mississippi, shows the conditions suffered by some of the poorest people in the United States.

◀ A combine harvester is used to harvest wheat on the Great Plains, near Casselton, North Dakota. The United States is the world's largest exporter of wheat.

AGRICULTURE

Agricultural activity in the United States occupies almost 20 per cent of the total land area. This highly efficient industry had sales worth over US$200 billion at the last agricultural census in 2002. The value of the industry has led to the growth of agri-business, in which farms are owned and run by companies or groups of investors rather than by farming families. There were nearly 74,000 such farms in 2002, but this is still a small number compared to the 1.9 million family or individually-run farms. A major trend in American agriculture over the last 70 years has been a reduction in the total number of farms, but an increase in their average size. In 1940 there were about six million farms with an average size of 67 hectares (166 acres), but today there are about two million farms and the average size has increased to 190 hectares (470 acres).

The main crops grown in the United States are soya beans, corn (maize), wheat, cotton and sorghum. Livestock production, especially beef, pork and poultry, is important and together with products such as eggs and milk accounts for 52.5 per cent of all agricultural sales.

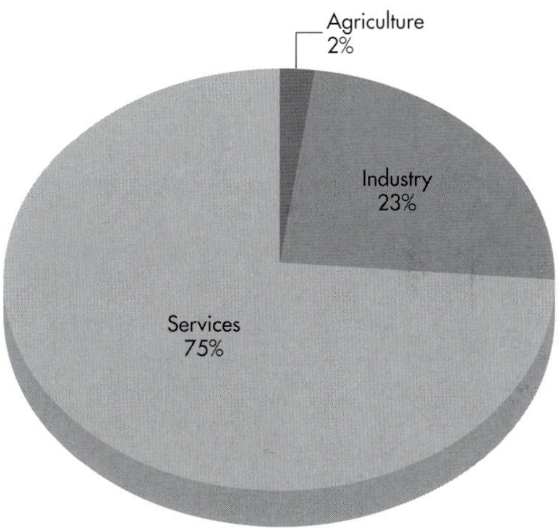

▲ Contribution by sector to national income

Economic data

- Gross National Income (GNI) in US$: 13,886,472,000,000
- World rank by GNI: 1
- GNI per capita in US$: 46,040
- World rank by GNI per capita: 15
- Economic growth: 2.2%

Source: World Bank

OLD AND NEW INDUSTRIES

Older industries that developed in the 19th century, such as steel production, are in decline, mainly due to competition from abroad where products can be made more cheaply. Many of the older, heavier industries are located in the east, in cities such as Pittsburgh, Pennsylvania, where there have been huge job losses in manufacturing. Pittsburgh is now developing high-tech industries such as computer software production in order to generate more work. However, the people who were employed in older industries often do not have the specific skills needed for these new jobs.

In the first eight months of 2005 there were 37,000 jobs lost in car manufacturing in the United States in response to a worldwide overproduction of cars. There were also 46,000 jobs lost in the textile industry as US firms moved their production overseas to less economically developed countries such as the Philippines, where labour costs are much cheaper. However, during the same time period over 500,000 new jobs were created in the service sector in the United States, many in tourism and retailing.

Focus on: Silicon Valley, California

Silicon Valley is the name given to an area located just south of San Francisco, California, where there is an important concentration of high-tech firms, such as Intel, Apple Computer and Hewlett-Packard. High-tech industries began to develop in the area in the 1950s, when Stanford University in San Francisco leased land to companies such as Varian Associates. Strong links were formed between the companies and the university's research departments, attracting more firms to the area. California's warm climate and pleasant living conditions continue to attract graduates from all over the world to work in Silicon Valley's cutting-edge industries.

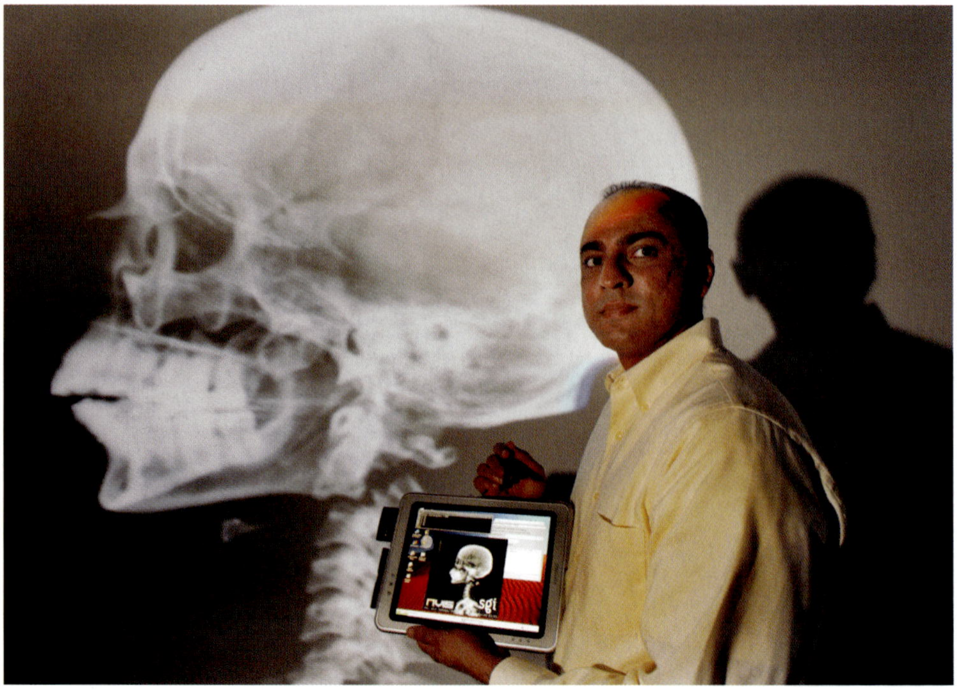

▶ Afshad Mistri of Silicon Graphics demonstrates how modern technology can help to determine the cause of a person's death by using special X-ray equipment to create a detailed cross-section of a body part. Many US companies lead the world in such cutting-edge research and development.

◀ Protestors hold up pink slips during an unemployment protest in Tempe, Arizona in 2004. The protest was held to draw attention to the economic policies of the then president, George W. Bush.

UNEMPLOYMENT

In 2005, eight million people were unemployed in the United States, which represents 5 per cent of the population. Several southern states had a higher than average unemployment rate, but some northern states where older industries are in decline also had a high rate, for example Michigan (7 per cent). The state with the lowest unemployment rate (2.7 per cent) was the island state of Hawaii, where there are many jobs in the tourist industry.

WEALTH AND POVERTY

In 2004, 12.7 per cent of the American population was living below the federal poverty line, which in 2003 was estimated to be US$26 a day per person. However, the distribution of poverty amongst different population groups is uneven. Over 25 per cent of African-Americans and 20 per cent of Hispanics live in poverty, compared to just 9 per cent of white Americans. In 2004, the average annual income per person in the United States was US$32,937. However, in Mississippi state, which has the highest percentage of African-Americans of any region in the United States (except for the District of Columbia where the capital, Washington, is located), the average annual income was over US$8,000 lower.

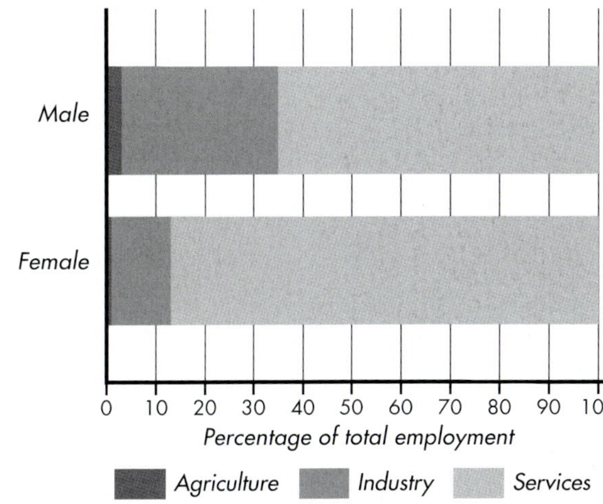

▲ Labour force by sector and gender

CHAPTER 8

Global Connections

As a leading world power, the United States has great influence through its foreign policies and military actions, its foreign trade relations, and through the exporting of its culture in the form of globally recognized brands, movies and television programmes.

GLOBALIZATION OR AMERICANIZATION?

Globalization refers to the process by which trade and business is increasingly conducted at a global scale and no longer depends on a company being located in its country of origin. Transnational companies (TNCs) have been largely responsible for the increasing globalization of the economy. They are firms that locate factories or services in several different countries in order to access cheaper labour or materials. TNCs may also be given tax incentives by governments as they help to create jobs and generate income in the host country.

An outcome of globalization is that TNCs market and sell their products around the world. American TNCs are especially strong in this area, with world-recognized brands such as the golden arches of McDonald's and the swoosh of Nike. In fact, US firms are so successful at marketing their products worldwide that some people talk about this as a process of Americanization rather than globalization.

▶ A film crew on location in Los Angeles, where the movie industry forms an important part of the city's economy. The popularity of Hollywood movies extends across the whole world.

Although this is good for US companies, the power these TNCs are able to exert in the market place has been criticized for pushing local alternatives out of business. For example, the media is one area in which the United States has particular dominance, with American television and movies being exported across the world. However, in Mexico the local film industry has all but disappeared due to the influx of Hollywood movies.

While the United States undoubtedly has an enormous influence on the world's media and economy, the process is not just one-way. For example, small, efficient cars produced in Japan, such as Toyota, have a good market in the United States. Japanese *manga* (comics) and *anime* (animation) are increasing in popularity in the United States, with many societies dedicated to viewing *anime*. And in the world of sport, soccer (football) has a growing fanbase in the United States as an alternative to the national sports of baseball and American football (see pages 52-3).

Did you know?

The US women's soccer team is one of the top three in world rankings.

Focus on: The Coca Cola Company

Coca Cola, one of America's most recognizable brands, is the largest private employer in Africa with over 60,000 employees. It is a transnational company that has contacts in over 200 countries worldwide, but whose headquarters are in Atlanta, Georgia in the United States. About 70 million Cola products are drunk in Africa every day, showing how popular the brand is.

FOREIGN TRADE

The United States' main trading partners are Canada, which accounts for 19.4 per cent of total trade in goods, and Mexico, which accounts for 11.3 per cent. Together, the three countries form a free-trade area called the North American Free Trade Agreement (NAFTA). NAFTA aims to reduce trade barriers between its three members and to form a trading group (or bloc) that can better compete with others, such as the European Union (EU).

▼ A Toyota technician shows a member of a First Aid squad how to disable the electronic motor of a Toyota Prius in case of an emergency. Japanese Toyota cars are increasingly popular in the United States.

▲ Containers of imported goods are unloaded at Long Beach, California.

IMPORTS AND EXPORTS

After Canada, the second biggest exporter to the United States is China. In 2006, the United States imported US$287.8 billion of goods from China, while it exported US$55.2 billion to China. This is known as a trade deficit. In fact, the United States has an overall trade deficit, and in 2006 it imported US$817.3 billion worth more of goods than it exported. The United States mainly imports oil, electrical goods and textiles as well as some foodstuffs. Apart from wheat, the United States is an important exporter of minerals, processed foods and drinks, vehicles and vehicle components, aeroplanes, technology and financial services.

? *Did you know?*

Through the United States Agency for International Development (USAID), the United States gives financial help to over 100 countries around the world.

INTERNATIONAL ROLES

As the world's only superpower, the United States plays a major role in many of the bodies that are involved in international affairs. The G8 is a group of eight developed-world countries, including the United States, that meets annually to discuss economic and political issues. In 2005, the group met at Gleneagles in Scotland where two of the main issues were development in Africa and climate change. The United States has only recently come into line with other countries and accepted that climate change is occurring as a result of human activities.

As a founder member of the United Nations (UN), the United States is influential in UN affairs. The UN tries to resolve conflicts by encouraging negotiation and disarmament, and sending peacekeeping troops to the world's troublespots. There is unease amongst some UN members about the United States' military intervention in 2003 in Iraq (see page 13) before full authorization by the UN Security Council, and countries such as France and Russia did not support this action. In 2002, North Korea admitted that it had nuclear weapons, and was developing nuclear reactors. The following year it withdrew from the Nuclear Non-proliferation Treaty (the international treaty that controls the spread of nuclear weapons). The United States, along with countries such as China, has been instrumental in trying to resolve this issue. In September 2005, North Korea re-signed the treaty and agreed to give up its nuclear activities.

◀ World leaders at the G8 Summit at Gleneagles in Scotland, July 2005. In the front row, second from left is the then president of the United States, George W. Bush. Tony Blair, at the prime minister of the UK, stands at the microphones.

Focus on: NATO

The North Atlantic Treaty Organization (NATO) is an alliance of 26 countries, including the United States, which was set up after the end of World War II in order to safeguard the freedom and security of its members by political or military means. Countries in NATO agree that an armed attack or threat to one of its members is regarded as an attack or threat against all members, and NATO would respond as a unit.

The United States is the largest country in this organization and arguably has the most power. Supporters of NATO suggest that this European-American alliance has helped in maintaining world peace because it represents a large proportion of the more economically developed world, and many countries would think very carefully before taking on such a force in a conflict.

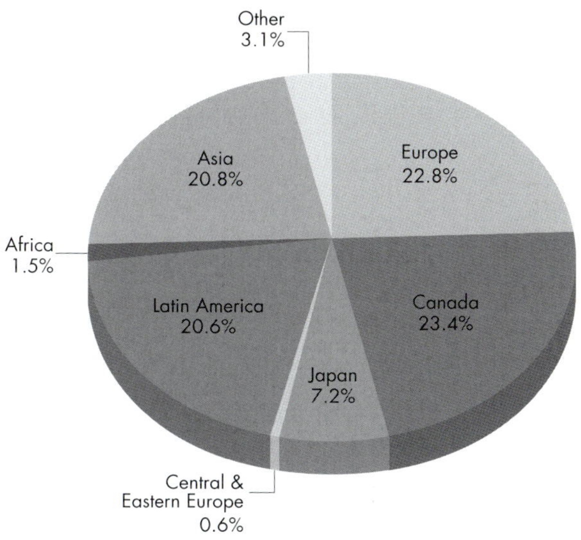

▲ Destination of exports by major trading region

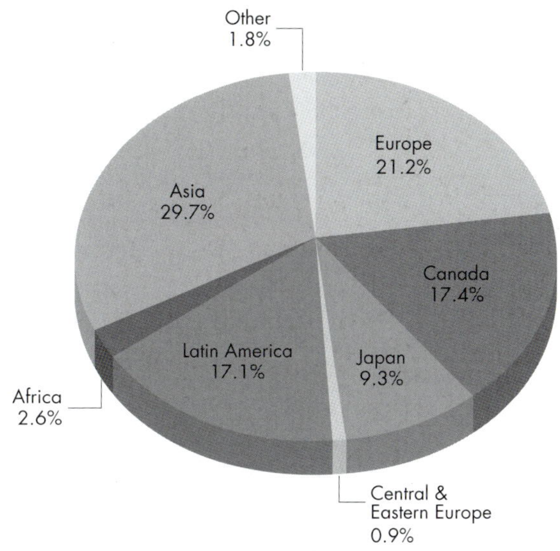

▲ Origin of imports by major trading region

CHAPTER 9

Transport and Communications

The huge size of the United States has led to the development of an extensive transport infrastructure (roads, railways, airports and ports) to cope with the distances involved in order for people and goods to move efficiently from one place to another. The distance between New York in the northeast of the country and Los Angeles in the southwest is 3,961 kilometres (2,462 miles) which is about the same distance as from London to the North Pole. Many people opt to fly between cities rather than take several days or weeks to travel across the country by road or rail.

ROAD AND RAIL

In the 19th century, the construction of the railroads helped to open up the west of the country by making transport to these distant lands accessible to all. Today, the railroads are much more important for carrying freight, such as wheat or iron ore. However, road transport still carries the majority of freight, as the railroads provide only limited access to many parts of the country. There are over 6 million kilometres (nearly 4 million miles) of roads, which trucks share with over 140 million cars. Cars are used for 90 per cent of all journeys over 50 miles, and only 1 per cent of such travellers use the train. With over one-third of American households having two cars, and a quarter having at least three, petrol consumption is high and there are environmental problems arising from car use, including air pollution and traffic congestion in many cities (see page 54).

Did you know?

The first electrically powered traffic lights in the world were introduced in Detroit, Michigan, in the 1920s, and were manually operated. The first automatic traffic lights appeared shortly after in Cleveland, Ohio.

◀ A driver on a Greyhound Line bus in Washington D.C. Greyhound bus routes link many American cities. After the terrorist attacks in 2001, the buses were fitted with new safety devices including a gate (left) to protect the driver from attacks by passengers.

AIR

There are 5,143 public-use airports in the United States and the nation has the largest number of airports and air connections in the world. Many of the flights are internal domestic flights, mainly between the big cities. The busiest airport in 2006 was Hartsfield Airport in Atlanta, Georgia, which had over 41 million passengers.

Focus on: Bay Area Rapid Transit (BART)

The city of San Francisco, a city of over 740,000 people on the west coast of the United States, suffers from air pollution from the car exhausts of its commuters. In 1974, the BART was opened. It is an electric railway, travelling above and below ground, which transports people to and from the suburbs and therefore reduces the amount of car use and air pollution. Journey times are much faster than by car, but the city is still having problems in encouraging more people to use this efficient system.

Transport & communications data

- Total roads: 6,430,366 km/ 3,995,644 miles
- Total paved roads: 4,165,110 km/ 2,588,079 miles
- Total unpaved roads: 2,265,256 km/ 1,407,565 miles
- Total railways: 226,612 km/ 140,810 miles
- Airports: 5,143
- Cars per 1,000 people: 814
- Mobile phones per 1,000 people: 839
- Personal computers per 1,000 people: 760
- Internet users per 1,000 people: 734

Source: World Bank and CIA World Factbook

▲ One of the 38 cable cars that run along three routes in San Francisco, California. This old-fashioned transport system is used mainly for carrying tourists.

Did you know?

The famous cable cars that ride up and down the hills of San Francisco, carrying thousands of tourists a week between the city centre and Fisherman's Wharf, are designated historical monuments.

WATER NETWORKS

The United States has 41,000 km (25,476 miles) of waterway and some routes are very important for trade. This is especially true of the Mississippi River which, with its tributaries and the Missouri River, provides a water route out of the Great Lakes region down to the Gulf ports in the south. Corn (maize), wheat and soya beans are transported down the river in large barges. Although slow, this form of transport is ideal for bulky, low-value goods as it is cheaper than transporting them by road. The United States' most important port is South Louisiana on the coast of the Gulf of Mexico. In 2007, 234 million tonnes (230 million tons) of goods moved through this port.

▼ Barges on the Mississippi River near Baton Rouge, Louisiana. Huge loads can be transported on these barges, which are towed by tugs.

THE MEDIA

The media plays a major role in the everyday lives of most Americans and there are over 13,000 radio stations, over 1,500 television stations, and about 9,000 cable networks. The Public Broadcasting Service (PBS) and National Public Radio (NPR) are run with the help of

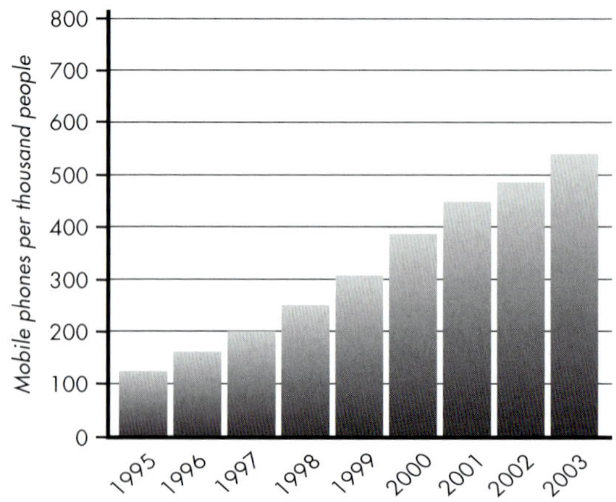

▲ Mobile phone use, 1995-2003

government funding, but all other channels are privately operated. There are more than 181 million telephone lines, more than 160 million cell phones (mobile phones) and about 163 million Internet users. US companies dominate the software needed for accessing the Internet and a few large companies such as AOL Times Warner, Disney and Viacom control most of the US media.

Although most Americans rate the television as their most reliable source of information, there are nevertheless more than 1,500 daily newspapers. Most of these cover mainly local issues with only the *Washington Post* and the *New York Times* giving in-depth coverage of matters of national concern. One of America's strengths is its emphasis on freedom of speech and freedom of the press, both of which are protected by the Constitution. These freedoms mean that Americans have the right to express their opinions in the media even when they disagree with the government of the day, without fear of prosecution.

Focus on: The development of the Internet

The Internet originated as a way of sharing information between a number of computers in different locations by the US military and the national government. The idea was further developed in the 1960s by research scientists at the Massachusetts Institute of Technology (MIT) who realized its potential for the transmission of knowledge. By the early 1970s, the first email program was written and the term 'Internet' began to be used. Private companies such as AOL became involved in the late 1980s, and the Internet quickly developed outside military and research use as the first commercial Internet Service Provider companies were formed.

▼ Access to computers has become increasingly important in education. In this new school, in Vail, Arizona, all students are supplied with laptops.

CHAPTER 10

Education and Health

The United States has well-developed education and health care systems, but access to these basic services is not equal for all people.

SCHOOLS

Although there is a federal Department of Education, most funding and supervision of education is under the control of individual states. The level of funding through local taxes is, therefore, a reflection of the wealth of a particular area, resulting in some areas being better provided for than others. Literacy rates are high, at 99 per cent for the whole country, but standards of literacy vary and low levels of literacy and numeracy remain problems for many adults at work, or seeking work. In 2002, the US government passed the No Child Left Behind Act, to improve standards in schools and specifically to encourage early reading and proficiency in maths. There are also state, workplace and voluntary programmes to address problems with adult literacy.

Did you know?

In 2005, 64 per cent of all American 3-5 year-olds (about eight million children) were enrolled in pre-school or nursery school.

All children in the United States receive at least 11 years of education, for which no fees are charged. Only 10 per cent of schools are private and most of these are linked to religious foundations. Most students attend elementary school (primary school) followed by middle school (called junior high school in some places), and then high school. Students may leave school at 16 although very few do, as it is difficult to get a job without having graduated from high school. Most students graduate from high school at about the age of 18.

High-school graduation rates vary between states. Many of those with low rates are southern states, such as Louisiana, Alabama and

◀ Graduating from high school is an important moment in a young person's life and is marked by ceremonies and parties. These students are celebrating at Stuart High, in Falls Church, Virginia.

Arkansas. This may reflect the racial make-up of the population, as completing high school is not always seen as a priority in some communities. In 2005 the national percentage of students completing high school nationally was 88 per cent. The completion rates for white students and black students are similar. However figures show that 27 per cent of Hispanic students did not graduate from high school.

HIGHER EDUCATION

In 2005 68 per cent of high school graduates (2.7 million students) went on to higher education in the United States. Higher education is expensive, however, and the majority of students have to combine their studying with jobs to earn money. Even so, many students graduate from their studies with debts of around US$40,000 which can take them many years to pay back. Higher education is available at local community colleges (where students can gain an associate degree after two years of study), state and private colleges, and universities (which award bachelors, masters and doctoral degrees).

Did you know?

Of the 191.9 million people in the United States aged over 25 in 2005, 86 per cent had a high school diploma, 27 per cent had a college degree and nearly 10 per cent had a postgraduate qualification.

Focus on: The Ivy League universities

The most prestigious universities in the United States, roughly equating to the UK's Oxford and Cambridge universities, are known as the Ivy League. It is said that the name comes from the ivy-clad walls of the universities involved. The league was originally linked to inter-university sports, but today these universities are renowned for the difficulty of gaining admission and their high academic standards. The eight universities in the League include Harvard University in Cambridge, Massachusetts, and Columbia University in New York City.

▲ Students outside part of the University of Columbia in New York City, which was founded in 1754 as King's College.

HEALTH CARE FOR THE MAJORITY

Health care in the United States is largely privately funded, and individuals are responsible for paying for their own health care. This is done either by taking out insurance policies or by receiving health insurance as a benefit from an employer. Health insurance is often offered as an incentive to attract a new employee to a job, and will usually cover the employee's family too. Having health insurance is important to most Americans because treatment for serious illness is expensive in the United States, as all aspects of health care have to be paid for including the hospital room, the services of the doctors, anaesthetists and nurses, the food, drugs and any tests carried out. This has led to a greater emphasis on preventative health care, and many Americans are very concerned with their health and fitness. There is a strong market for vitamins and other dietary supplements in order to improve well-being.

Did you know?

As the nation has become wealthier, levels of obesity have increased in children. Between 1976 and 1980 only 6 per cent of children were obese but by 2002 this figure had risen to 16 per cent.

UNEVEN ACCESS

For those on low incomes there is a government scheme called Medicaid which provides some form of health insurance for 38 million people, as well as long-term care for 12 million elderly and disabled. Although the largest group receiving Medicaid comprises parents and children from low-income families (75 per cent), the greatest amount of spending is on the elderly, who absorb 70 per cent of the funding. However, there are many people who are neither insured nor eligible to receive Medicaid – 44.8 million in 2005, which is more than 15 per cent of the population. As the cost of health care continues to rise and the number of people without insurance also grows, there are concerns that planned government cuts to the Medicaid scheme will affect the most vulnerable people in US society.

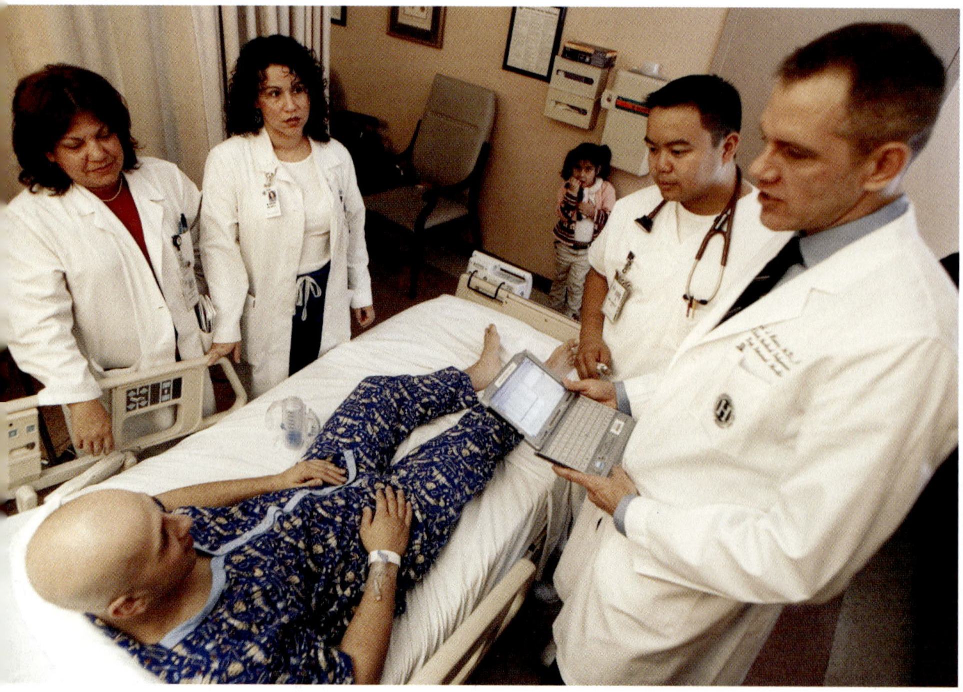

◀ A doctor reviews a patient's progress with other medical professionals at the Hackensack Medical Center, New Jersey.

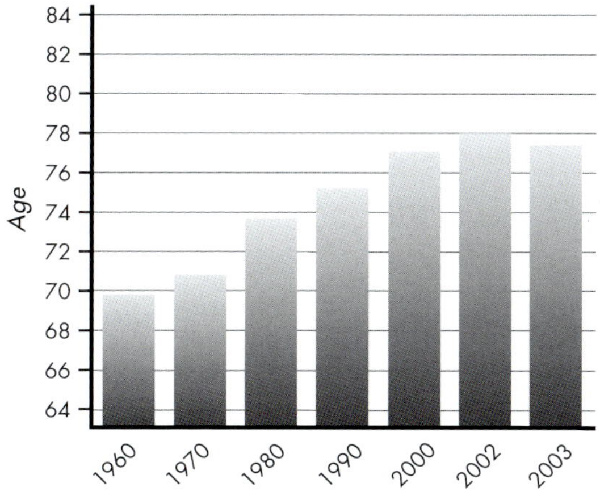

▲ Life expectancy at birth 1960-2003

Education and health

- Life expectancy at birth male: 75.3
- Life expectancy at birth female: 81.1
- Infant mortality rate per 1,000: 6
- Under five mortality rate per 1,000: 8
- Physicians per 1,000 people: 2
- Health expenditure as % of GDP: 15.4%
- Education expenditure as % of GDP: 5.9%
- Primary net enrolment: 92%
- Pupil-teacher ratio, primary: 14
- Adult literacy as % age 15+: 99%

Source: United Nations Agencies and World Bank

Focus on: Obesity in the United States

One of the most pressing health problems in the United States is that of obesity and subsequent complications such as diabetes. Over 65 per cent of the population is overweight, and 31 per cent is classed as obese. Reasons for this level of obesity include a diet that features a lot of cheap fast food, which is high in calories and saturated fats, and also the fact that many people are increasingly car-dependent and not willing to walk or take regular exercise. It is thought that the rise in obesity will lead to an increase in the incidence rates of diabetes, heart disease, breathing problems, cancer and serious joint problems. Each year 300,000 people in the United States die prematurely as a result of being overweight.

◀ A fitness instructor leads an exercise class at Linden, New Jersey.

CHAPTER 11

Culture and Religion

The United States has often been referred to as a 'melting pot' of many different peoples and cultures. Since the birth of the United States, the flow of immigrants from all over the world has resulted in a rich cross-fertilisation of ideas and traditions that has given the United States its own unique culture. For example, early French settlers in Louisiana transferred their musical heritage, gave it an American twist and the result was Cajun music. The African slaves who came to the United States brought with them the sounds and rhythms of their native music which later developed into blues and jazz (see box).

International origins also show in the vast range of festivals that Americans celebrate today. Some are purely American, such as Independence Day on 4 July which marks the declaration of independence by the 13 colonies (see page 9), and Thanksgiving (see page 8).

Focus on: Jazz

Jazz music is one of America's most distinctive cultural creations. The music developed in part from the rhythms and musical heritage that black slaves brought with them from Africa. Early in the history of jazz, New Orleans was the centre of the jazz community. By the 1930s, jazz was played and enjoyed by both blacks and whites. Some of the greatest jazz musicians include Charlie Parker, Miles Davis, John Coltrane and Thelonious Monk.

◀ Bagpipe players from the US Marine Corps march past St Patrick's Cathedral during the St Patrick's Day parade in New York, 17 March 2001.

Others relate to the many cultures that make up the population such as the St Patrick's Day parades on 17 March in cities with Irish-American communities, particularly Boston and New York, or the Calle Oche Festival in Miami, Florida, which is held every March and celebrates Hispanic culture and heritage in the largest street party in the world.

NATIVE AMERICAN CULTURE

Native Americans make up only 1 per cent of the population of the United States, but many Native Americans remain determined to maintain their ancient cultures and way of life. Several of the larger Native American groups organize regular gatherings, or pow-wows, in order to celebrate Native American music, dance and crafts and to study their history. Today, the largest Native American tribe is the Navajo. Members of the Navajo live in their own nation, which spreads across parts of the three states of Utah, New Mexico and Arizona, with their own elected government. Although they live under most of the same laws as other American citizens, the Navajo have their own police and schools, set their own taxes, and speak their own language, combining modern life with their rich cultural heritage.

▼ A pow-wow at Cashmere, Washington State, offers members of different Native American tribes the chance to celebrate their cultures and traditions.

RELIGION AND THE STATE

There is no state religion in the United States and the Constitution allows citizens to have the freedom to worship (or not) as they please. Whilst in state schooling, many American schoolchildren say the Pledge of Allegiance to the US flag (see page 5), but there are no religious ceremonies within the school day.

▼ The congregation leaves a Baptist church after a service in Beaufort, South Carolina. Baptists are the major Christian denomination in the United States, especially in the southern states.

All past US presidents have professed a Christian-based religion, and, in 2007, over 75 per cent of the population declared themselves to be Christians. Reflecting the origins of many of the early European settlers, Protestant Christianity still accounts for over 33 per cent of Christian believers with Roman Catholics accounting for about 25 per cent. The Baptists form the largest group within the Protestant Church, and are particularly strong in the southern states, often known as the 'Bible Belt'. The Church plays a major role in many communities, not just as a place of worship but also as a centre for the social life of many communities. The United States is home to about 6 million Jews – the largest Jewish population outside the state of Israel. The country's greatest concentration of Jews is in New York.

One of the fastest-growing religions in the United States is Islam. Most of this growth has been in the African-American community, which now makes up about 42 per cent of American Muslims. There are over 1,000 mosques in the country, the large majority in metropolitan areas.

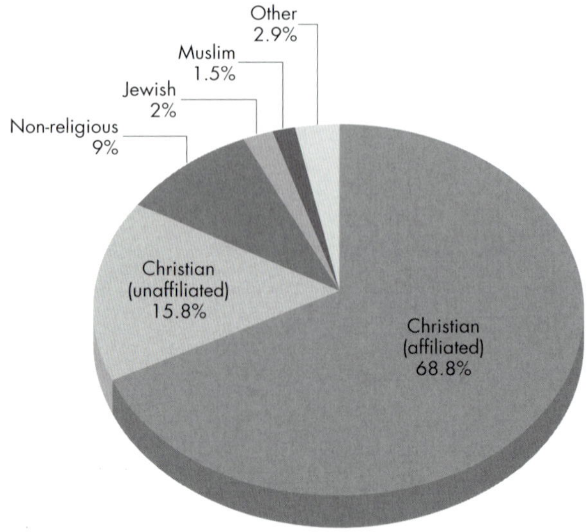

▲ America's major religions

In 2001, nearly 26 million people (9 per cent) said they were not affiliated to any religion – an increase of 6 per cent since 1990. Today, increasing numbers are turning away from traditional religions and trying to find alternative beliefs that answer their questions. Some of the new interests reflect far older beliefs, including Eastern religions such as Buddhism, and pagan religions.

NEW RELIGIONS

During the 19th century, several new religious groups were created in the United States. Two of the better-known, the Church of Latter Day Saints (often referred to as the Mormons) and Jehovah's Witnesses, are essentially branches of the Christian Church. Both of these organizations have spread worldwide from their beginnings in the United States. The Mormons were founded by Joseph Smith, with beliefs based on the *Book of Mormon* that Smith reported had been revealed to him. They eventually moved west to avoid persecution and settled in Utah, in what is now Salt Lake City, the present-day location of their headquarters. There are estimated to be over 3 million Mormons in the United States. Jehovah's Witnesses believe in the imminent return of Jesus Christ and preach this belief door-to-door. There are nearly 2 million Jehovah's Witnesses in the United States.

▼ Dr Amina Wadud leads a group of women at the first public, mixed-gender Muslim prayer service, held in New York City in March 2005.

CHAPTER 12

Leisure and Tourism

The average American works hard for a living, spending more hours at work and having less vacation time than the average European. This means that leisure time is especially valued in the United States. It is common, for example, for families to go camping for just a couple of days at the weekend so that they can spend time together. With such short vacations it is difficult to travel long distances, and this may explain why it is estimated that only 20 per cent of the US population has a passport for travel abroad. The United States also has such a lot to offer within its borders, with a huge choice of holiday destinations to attract people, ranging from long, sandy beaches and the scenery of its deserts and mountains to historic and vibrant cities such as New York and San Francisco.

THE TOURISM INDUSTRY

The tourism industry in the United States is worth US$99 billion and is therefore very important to the country's economy. There are 2.6 million hotel rooms sold every day in the United States, supporting hundreds of thousands of jobs. Revenue from tourism is also important to the US economy and contributes towards public spending through the taxes tourists pay on goods and services. If tourism were to collapse then it is estimated that each American household would need to pay around US$898 in taxes to prevent public budgets from falling.

▼ A family enjoys a wilderness camping expedition in the Sawtooth National Forest, Idaho.

With most employees having only two weeks vacation a year, the vast majority of people holiday within the United States, often within their own state. Outdoor holidays are popular. In the winter there are many fabulous ski resorts in the Rocky Mountains and elsewhere, and the warm climate of Florida attracts visitors to its beaches all year round. Many families visit attractions such as Disneyland near Los Angeles, and Disneyworld in Florida. When Americans do travel abroad, the most popular destination is Western Europe (40 per cent of all visits) and the most visited country is the UK (14 per cent of all overseas visits).

Focus on: Las Vegas

Las Vegas lies in the middle of the desert in Nevada state. The city celebrated its 100th birthday in 2005. In its short history it has become the gambling capital of the world, and in 2007 it attracted over 39 million visitors. The huge casino resorts that line the Strip (the main thoroughfare) offer 24-hour gambling tables and slot machines as well as restaurants, high-class shopping and extravagant shows. So much money is earned by the city in its casinos that there is no state income tax in Nevada.

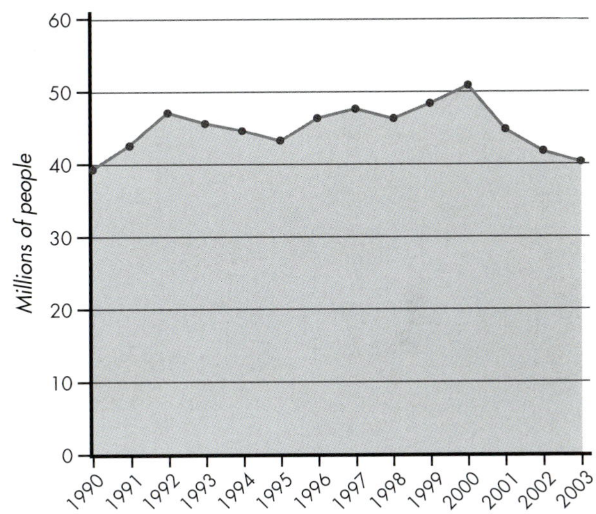

▲ Changes in international tourism, 1990-2003

Did you know?

There are approximately 7.3 million people employed in the tourism industry in the United States.

◀ A killer whale performs for an audience at SeaWorld Adventure Park, one of several theme parks located around Orlando, Florida.

▲ Skiiers enjoy the snow at the Deer Valley Ski Resort, Utah.

VISITORS TO AMERICA

In 2006, over 50 million overseas visitors came to the United States. The three states that received the most overseas visitors were New York, Florida and California. New York City is the top all-year-round tourist destination, offering world-famous sights such as the Statue of Liberty, the Empire State Building and Central Park as well as numerous internationally recognized museums, theatres and art galleries. Both federal and state governments invest money in marketing the United States as a holiday destination because of the importance of creating and maintaining a wide range of jobs.

Did you know?

Rollerblades or in-line skates were developed in the 1980s by two American ice-hockey players in order to continue practising their skating technique even when there was no ice.

LEISURE

Over 95 per cent of people in the United States spend an average of five hours a day on sport or leisure, with watching television accounting for about three hours per day. Other important leisure activities include shopping – a visit to the local mall is often a social as well as a retail activity – as well as a wide range of hobbies and cultural activities such as going to the movies, or to an event such as an exhibition or a concert.

SPORTS

The United States is a great sporting nation. In the Summer Olympics of 2008, the United States was the most successful team overall, winning 110 medals – of which 36 were gold. Sports such as American football, basketball and baseball are played at school, in the local community and professionally, and generate huge amounts of enthusiasm and support. If a student is successful at high-school level in one of these sports, it is possible to secure a valuable

Tourism in the United States

- Tourist arrivals, millions: 50.978
- Earnings from tourism in US$: 128,922,000,000
- Tourism as % foreign earnings: 9%
- Tourist departures, millions: 63.662
- Expenditure on tourism in US$: 104,310,000,000

Source: World Bank

scholarship and play for a university team at the same time as contining his or her studies. Famous baseball and basketball teams include the New York Yankees (baseball) and the Los Angeles Lakers (basketball). Ice hockey is also popular, particularly in the eastern states. Successful athletes and sportspeople such as Tiger Woods (golf) and Peyton Manning (American football) can command high salaries, and lucrative sponsorship deals add to their wealth and celebrity.

Motor car racing has large numbers of fans in the United States, particularly stock car racing which is hugely popular as a spectator sport at race tracks across the country and on television. The National Association for Stock Car Auto Racing (NASCAR) oversees the sport and runs its three major events: the NEXTEL Cup Series, the Busch Series and the Craftsman Truck Series. The United States is host to several important international sporting fixtures including major golf tournaments and the US Open (tennis). Soccer is also becoming increasingly popular (see page 35).

Did you know?

In the 1970s an east-coast surfer developed the first board for use on snow. Snowboarding became popular in the late 1980s and it became an Olympic sport in 1998.

Focus on: Baseball

Baseball is generally regarded as the national game of the United States. The game is thought to have been adapted from the English game of rounders, although baseball is much more energetic. Children play baseball in the Little League, and most parks in the United States have at least one baseball field. The game received professional status in 1871 and since then the national major league championship for baseball has been called the World Series. No team has been more successful than the New York Yankees, who by 2004 had won the World Series 26 times.

▼ A capacity crowd watches an American football match between the New York Jets and the Indianapolis Colts at the Giant's Stadium, New Jersey.

CHAPTER 13

Environment and Conservation

The United States' high levels of economic development have come at some cost to its environment. Although there is a much greater understanding of the impact of human activities on natural environments in the United States today, many areas are still under pressure from resource extraction or misuse. In 1892, the influential Sierra Club was created by John Muir in California to encourage the protection of the wild spaces in the United States. The Sierra Club was instrumental in setting up the first national parks and today it plays an important role in raising awareness of human impacts on natural surroundings. More modern pressure groups such as Friends of the Earth and Greenpeace began in the United States during the second half of the 20th century, and have worked to highlight what they see as gross misuse of resources and land.

SOIL EROSION

Intensive agriculture, especially in the Midwest states, has led to some areas of soil being ploughed and left unvegetated. During times of heavy rainfall in these areas exposed topsoil is washed away, gradually reducing the fertility of the land. Farmers have addressed this problem through the use of chemical fertilizers, but excessive use of these fertilizers has itself made the soil more crumbly and prone to removal by wind, adding to the problem.

AIR POLLUTION AND ACID RAIN

Although air quality has improved in the United States as a whole over the last 30 years, it continues to deteriorate in US cities such as Los Angeles as a result of high car use and the resulting pollutants from exhausts. Problems with air quality have led to increased numbers of respiratory problems in the population as a whole, and cause 159,000 trips to hospital emergency rooms and over six million asthma attacks each summer. The regions most heavily

◄ The Californian city of Los Angeles is often shrouded in smog, caused by exhaust emissions from the millions of vehicles that travel along its roads.

affected are Los Angeles, the Houston-Galveston area in the south and the heavily urbanized northeast of the United States.

Emissions from car and factory exhausts produce sulphur dioxide and nitrogen dioxide which, when dissolved in rainfall, cause acid rain. Acid rain affects the ability of forest trees to absorb nutrients through their roots and to photosynthesize efficiently. The trees' leaves turn yellow, and the trees may eventually die. The pollutants are often carried by the wind away from the area producing them, to fall as rain in a distant area. The northeast, for example the Green Mountains in Vermont, is particularly affected by acid rain, but the problem also crosses the US-Canada border. In 1991, Canada and the United States signed an Air Quality Agreement to reduce the levels of acid rain by using filters on factory and power station chimneys, and already there has been a reduction of over a third in emissions.

Environmental and conservation data

- Forested area as % total land area: 27%
- Protected area as % total land area: 15.8%
- Number of protected areas: 7,448

SPECIES DIVERSITY

Category	*Known species*	*Threatened species*
Mammals	428	37
Breeding birds	508	55
Reptiles	360	27
Amphibians	283	25
Fish	1,101	130
Plants	19,473	169

Source: World Resources Institute

▼ The forests on Mount Mitchell in North Carolina show evidence of damage from acid rain, with branches stripped of foliage and some dead trees.

PROTECTING THE NATURAL HERITAGE

Much of the natural environment of the United States has some protection at either a local, state or national level. Included at a national level are parks, seashores, rivers and lake shores.

There are 52 national parks, run by the National Parks Service, which cover landscapes as varied as the Rocky Mountains, desert areas of the southwest, and tundra regions in Alaska. The aim is both to protect the environment of the parks and at the same time allow access to visitors to enjoy the parks' natural beauty. The first national park was Yellowstone, Wyoming, which was set up in 1872 to protect its volcanic landscape. People still come from around the world to view its geysers and boiling pools and, like the Grand Canyon National Park, Yellowstone attracts over 4 million visitors a year. Other national parks include the arctic tundra of Denali National Park, the rocky coastline and forest of Acadia National Park in Maine, the dramatic Canyonlands in Utah and the swamplands of the Everglades in Florida.

Did you know?

Ninety per cent of the wood in New Orleans' historic French Quarter is infested with the Formosan termite, an imported alien species, and millions of dollars are spent in pest control every year. The termites arrived in the wood of packing crates from Southeast Asia, 60 years ago.

▼ Wilderness areas in national parks are vital to protect both habitats and species such as this mountain lion, photographed in Canyonlands National Park, Utah.

THE ARCTIC NATIONAL WILDLIFE REFUGE

In the United States, near the border with Canada, is the Arctic National Wildlife Refuge, an important area for caribou (reindeer). It is an isolated area and its wildlife thrives away from human interference. However, its protection is now in doubt as there is increasing pressure for oil and gas exploration to take place. Environmentalists fear that this activity will interfere with the breeding and migration of the caribou herds and damage the fragile ecosystems of the tundra for many years to come. Environmentalists argue that Americans should aim to reduce their fossil fuel use before exploiting such unique and fragile areas.

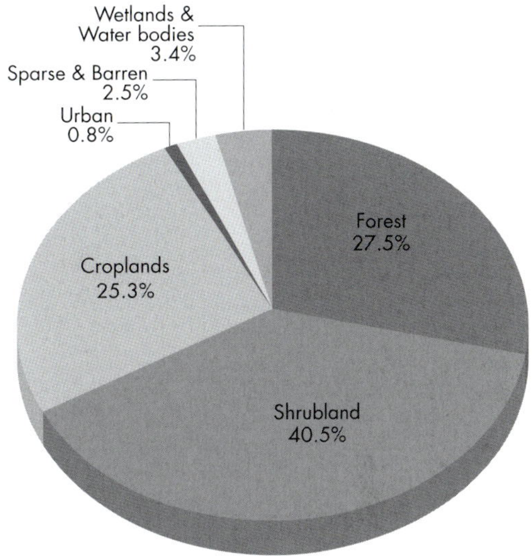

▲ Types of habitat

Focus on: Alien invaders

It is estimated that about 6,000 alien (non-native) plant and animal species have entered the United States through human activity. These alien species often cause problems because they do not have any natural predators in their new home. The tamarisk is an alien tree, introduced from Europe in the 19th century as an ornamental plant. It has spread from the parks, where it was originally planted, along riverbanks, especially in the southwest, where it shades out the native cottonwoods and willows. This has reduced the habitat for native birds and animals and changed the ecosystem. Now, volunteers go out 'tammy bashing' at weekends – pulling up the young trees in order to reduce the problem.

◀ Children from the city of Miami, Florida, learn about wildlife from a ranger in the Everglades National Park.

CHAPTER 14

Future Challenges

The United States is an immensely wealthy and powerful nation, but it has a number of problems that it must face during the 21st century as both its economy and position in world politics change.

INTERNATIONAL RELATIONS

Since the terrorist attacks in September 2001, the United States has taken a more active line against countries, particularly Islamic states, that it perceives as a threat. This has increased tensions between the US government and countries such as Iran. Relationships with many Muslim and Arab nations are also strained because of the United States' involvement in the Middle East, particularly in Iraq. Another source of tension is the United States' continuing support for the state of Israel, although the United States has played a major role in pushing forward the peace process between Israel and the Palestinians. The United States is also involved in countering the potential nuclear threat posed by countries such as North Korea (see page 36) and Iran.

The 'war against terrorism' will continue to be a challenge. In 2002, as a direct result of the terrorist attacks of the previous year, the US government created a new department for 'Homeland Security' which is charged with protecting people and property from harm and damage. However, the first major challenge to the new department came not from terrorism, but from Hurricane Katrina in 2005 (see page 15), demonstrating that the United States needs to improve dramatically its ability to respond to catastrophic events (see box).

The United States' involvement in conflicts in other countries is having an impact on its economy. In 2006, US$546 billion was spent on the US military budget, and some commentators have questioned whether a continuation of this level of spending is viable.

◀ Young Americans from diverse ethnic backgrounds show pride in their shared national identity.

With the rise of other world groupings, such as a united and expanded Europe, and the fast economic growth of both China and India, it may be that the dominance of the United States as the world's only superpower could be challenged in the future.

GROWING DISPARITIES

One of the major challenges for domestic policy is to address the increasing gap between rich and poor in the United States. The United Nations calculates that the wealthiest 10 per cent of Americans enjoy 30 per cent of the country's wealth, whereas the poorest 10 per cent share less than 2 per cent. Young people who leave school without skills or qualifications are less likely to obtain jobs, especially in the new high-tech industries which is where most economic growth lies. They are also likely to have problems accessing health care. Several government programmes are being developed to tackle these problems. For example, Reading First gives federal funding to the states with the aim of encouraging early readers (see page 42). Other funding is available to improve students' IT expertise.

Providing more Americans with the skills and opportunities to better share in their country's wealth and success could help to reduce the United States' growing disparities. In addition, a fairer distribution of wealth could result in a fall in crime levels and the growth of a more cohesive society. All of this would help to fulfil the ideals put forward by the writers of the Constitution (see page 9) to create a: 'more perfect union, establish Justice and ensure domestic tranquillity'.

Focus on: Defence against natural disaster

After the devastating hurricane damage of 2004 and 2005, a future challenge is to protect vulnerable communities along America's coasts. The main threats are the danger of tsunamis along the Pacific coast in the west and hurricanes along the coasts of the southeast and the Gulf of Mexico. More than half the population (153 million) of the United States lives on or near the coast and research into better and faster evacuation of these areas needs to be carried out.

◀ The future for fuel? An electric vehicle passes through an alternative fuel station in San Diego, California, where customers can fill up with a range of fuels from petrol to natural gas.

Timeline

c.8000 BC Migration of people from Asia to America across landbridge.

c.1000 AD Viking explorer Leif Erikson reaches North America.

1492 Christopher Columbus makes landfall in the Bahamas and discovers the 'New World'.

1607 First English colony founded at Jamestown, West Virginia.

1620 Pilgrim Fathers (Puritans) found Plymouth Colony in Massachusetts.

1733 There are now 13 British colonies.

1763 End of war with France in America. Britain controls Canada and all land east of the Mississippi River in North America.

1773 Date of the Boston Tea Party when colonists rebelled against being taxed by Britain.

1776 4 July, Declaration of Independence.

1781 British surrender at Yorktown, Virginia.

1783 War of Independence against Britain ends officially with signing of the Treaty of Paris.

1789 George Washington elected president of the United States.

1803 Louisiana purchased from France.

1861-5 Civil War between the northern 'Union' states and the southern 'Confederate' states.

1865 President Abraham Lincoln is assassinated.

1867 Alaska purchased from Russia.

1917 The United States joins World War I on the side of the Allies.

1929 Wall Street stock market crash.

1929-39 Great Depression

1941 Pearl Harbor bombing. The United States enters World War II.

1945 American planes drop atomic bombs on the Japanese cities of Hiroshima and Nagasaki, ending the war in the Pacific.

1945-89 Cold War with the Soviet Union.

1950-3 Korean War.

1963 Start of Vietnam war (until 1973).

1973-4 Oil-crisis as OPEC countries limit oil exports.

1980s Period of economic growth.

1990-1 Gulf War. The United States leads a coalition to liberate Kuwait from the Iraqis.

1992 Democrat Bill Clinton elected as president.

2001 Republican G.W. Bush elected as president.

2001 11 September, terrorist attacks in New York and Washington D.C.

2001 October, the United States leads retaliatory action against the Taliban rulers of Afghanistan, where terrorists are thought to be trained.

2003 The United States invades Iraq to remove Saddam Hussein from power and replace his regime with a democratically elected government. War officially ends in May 2003 but conflict continues.

2004 November, G.W. Bush is re-elected.

2005 September, Hurricane Katrina devastates Louisiana, particularly the city of New Orleans.

Glossary

Acid rain Rainfall that contains sulphur dioxide and nitrogen oxides from exhaust gases, making it more acidic than normal.

Agribusiness Large-scale, commercial farming.

Baptists Members of a Christian Church who believe in adult baptism by immersion in water.

Census An official gathering of information about a population in a certain area, often carried out at intervals of ten years.

Civil rights The rights of a citizen to liberty and equality. Used particularly with reference to African-Americans' search to achieve these rights.

Communism A political system that abolishes private ownership and emphasizes common ownership of property and the means of production.

Confederacy The southern slave states in the American Civil War (1861-5).

Democracy A political system in which representatives are chosen by the people in free elections.

Ecosystem A particular area consisting of living organisms (plants, animals etc.) and the physical environment that surrounds them.

Emissions Waste gases and particles given out from factory chimneys and car exhausts.

Federal The centralized government of the United States, separate from the state governments.

Free enterprise An economic system in which businesses are allowed to be free from state or government control.

Geothermal Describes energy that is generated by the earth's core which can be tapped by humans via hot rocks or water. It can either be used directly, or harnessed to generate electricity.

Globalization The process by which trade and business is increasingly conducted at a global scale.

Gross National Product (GNP) The total value of all goods and services produced annually by a nation.

High-tech industries Industries that use the latest techniques and technology – usually referring to telecommunications, electronics and IT.

Hispanic Describes a person originating from Spanish-speaking cultures in Central or South America, Puerto Rico, Cuba or Mexico.

Hurricane A tropical cyclone which begins out at sea and moves inland with wind speeds exceeding 120 km per hour (75 mph).

Levee A barrier to protect against flooding.

Market economy An economy based on supply and demand, with little or no government control.

Migrant A person who moves away from their home or country.

Naturalization The process of becoming a citizen of a country.

Photosynthesis The process by which green plants build up sugars using solar energy, carbon dioxide and water.

Photovoltaic The use of the sun's energy to create an electric current.

Prairie The large plain in the centre of North America which was originally grassland.

Stock market The place where company stocks and shares are traded.

Sustainable Using resources in a way that preserves them for the future.

Tectonic plate One of the large areas of the earth's crust which lie on top of the molten rock beneath.

Tornado A violent, revolving storm that forms over heated land.

Trade deficit When a country imports more goods (in terms of value) than it exports.

Transnational Companies (TNCs) Companies that have their headquarters in one country and production units in other nations.

Tributary A river that joins a larger river.

Tundra A treeless area found at high latitudes where the dominant vegetation is made up of grasses, lichens and mosses.

Union The northern free states in the American Civil War (1861-5).

Urban sprawl The uncontrolled growth of an urban area.

Further Information

BOOKS TO READ

Access to History: Race Relations in the USA since 1900
Vivienne Saunders
(Hodder Education, 2003)

Access to History: The American Civil War 1861-65
Alan Farmer
(Hodder Education, 2002)

Countries of the World: The USA
Sally Garrington
(Evans, 2002)

Twentieth-century History Makers: Martin Luther King
Anita Ganeri and Nicola Barber
(Watts, 2003)

NOVELS
Al Capone Does my Shirts
Gennifer Choldenko
(Putnam, 2005)
Set on Alcatraz where the father of the main character works. Light-hearted but also looks at issues of imprisonment and compassion.

Kira-Kira
Cynthia Kadohata
(Simon and Schuster, 2005)
Set in the 1950s and '60s in the south of the United States. The story is about a Japanese American family and how they cope in the racially segregated south.

USEFUL WEBSITES

http://quickfacts.census.gov/qfd/states/00000.html
Facts on population, education, households etc. for the United States as a whole, and individual states.

http://odur.let.rug.nl/~usa/GEO/homepage.htm
A brief regional geography of the United States produced by the United States Information Agency.

http://www.america.gov
A portrait of the United States. Background to many aspects of life in the United States.

http://www.doi.gov
Department of the Interior site with many useful links including the National Parks Service, the Bureau of Indian Affairs and the US Geological Service. There are also links to webcams at locations such as the Grand Canyon and the geyser, Old Faithful, in Yellowstone National Park.

http://www.census.gov
Huge database with access to many interesting articles.

http://www.navajo.org/
The Navajo nation website.

Index

Page numbers in **bold** indicate pictures.

About the Author

Sally Garrington is an experienced teacher of geography and a senior examiner for a major exam board. She has written books on the United States and Canada and regularly organizes geographical study visits to the USA.